Tefal EasyFry Air Fryer & Grill Cookbook

365-Day Delicious, Easy, and Fast Air Fryer Recipes to Make Your Life Easy and Making Delicious Meals.

Albu Jacob

Table of Contents

Introduction 7

Chapter 1: Appetizers and Snacks Recipes.................8

Sweet Potato Wedges.. 9

Air Fryer Burger 9

Holiday Beef Patties... 10

Air Fryer Halloumi 11

Potato Slices 12

Chicken Nuggets.. 13

Carrot Cake.. 14

Air Fryer Tofu 15

White Mushrooms Appetizer 15

Chicken Drumsticks 16

Polenta Biscuits 17

Kale and Celery Crackers 18

Boiled Eggs 18

Cheesy Chicken Wings 19

Squash Pate 20

Shrimp and Calamari Snack 21

Potato and Beans Dip 22

Chapter 2: Breakfast Recipes 24

Breakfast Potatoes 25

Air Fryer Falafel 26

Two Ingredient Pizza 27

Frozen Sausage Rolls 28

Mashed Potato Balls 29

Air Fryer Pizza 30

Cheese Biscuits 31

Hash Browns 31

Pizza Scrolls 32

Roast Potatoes 33

Mashed Potatoes 34

Potato Wedges 35

Chapter 3: Poultry Recipes 37

Chicken Thighs 38

Piri Piri Chicken Legs 38

Chicken Breast 39

Buffalo Wings 40

Cajun Chicken 42

Chicken Tenders 42

Rotisserie Chicken 44

Chicken Nachos 45

Fried Chicken 45

Chicken Breasts 47

Hunters Chicken 48

Chicken Parmesan 49

BBQ Chicken Breast 50

Spicy Chicken Thighs 51

Chapter 4: Meats Recipes 53

Steak Bites 54

Air Fryer Sausages 55

Frozen Sausages 55

Air Fryer Bacon 56

Sirloin Steak 57

Mozzarella-Stuffed Meatballs 58

Air Fryer Meatballs 59

Frozen Steak In Air Fryer 60

Crispy Air Fryer Bacon 61

Air Fryer Steak 61

Lamb Chops 62

Pork Chops 63

Chapter 5: Vegetable Recipes 65

Air Fryer Parsnips 66

Brussel Sprouts 66

Carrot Fries 67

Garlic and Herb Potatoes 68

Artichokes and Mayonnaise 69

Hasselback Potatoes 70

Zucchini with Mozzarella 71

Grilled Asparagus with Sauce 72

Spicy Thai–Style Veggies 73

Parsnips Recipe (Honey Glazed) 74

Air Fryer Onions 74

Simple Green Beans 75

Grille Tomatoes with Herb Salad 76

Roasted Tomatoes 77

Simple Grilled Vegetables 78

Eggplant Mix 79

Spicy Kale Mix 80

Chapter 6: Desserts Recipes 81

Chocolate Brownies 82

Air Fryer Cookies 83

Dessert Pizza 84

Apple Turnovers 85

Peanut Butter Cookies 86

Chocolate Chip Cookies 88

Fruit Scones 89

Cinnamon Rolls 90

Air Fryer Brownies 91

Apricot and Raisin Cake 92

Air Fryer Pizookie 93

Chapter 7: Wraps and Sandwiches Recipes 95

Ham Hock Calzone Pizza 96

Sausage Rolls 97

Hot Dogs 98

Ham Hock and Spring Greens Hash 99

Carrot and Orange Traybake 100

Prawn Toast 101

Roast Plum and Rhubarb Meringue Pots 102

Grilled Rump Steak Sandwich 104

Camembert Wedges with Cranberry Sauce 105

Fish Finger Sandwiches with Fresh Tartar Sauce 106

INTRODUCTION

I f you're seeking a flexible and healthier way to prepare food at home, Tefal's EasyFry line is a must-have.

You can enjoy health-conscious cooking with 99% less oil thanks to this combination of air fryer and grill. It offers quick outcomes and uses less energy than a conventional oven. Meals may be prepared for up to six people in the spacious capacity, and the die-cast grill plate will perfectly sear meat without the use of additional fat.

This cookbook is an amazing collection of yummy recipes that are specifically designed for your Tefal EasyFry Air Fryer & Grill. Everything you need to get started is right here inside this cookbook. You can make mouthwatering dishes only by using ingredients in your hand.

Cook an immense variety of recipes and spend days cooking non-stop with your favorite kitchen appliance!

Chapter 1: Appetizers and Snacks Recipes

Sweet Potato Wedges

Preparation Time: 10 Minutes
Cook Time: 20 Minutes
Serves: 4

Ingredients:

- Salt and pepper according to taste
- 1 tablespoon oil (olive oil)
- 1 teaspoon smoked paprika
- 1 teaspoon garlic powder
- 4 large sweet potatoes

Directions:

1. Preheat the air fryer to 200°C.
2. Prepare the sweet potatoes by chopping off the ends and cleaning them.
3. Slice them lengthwise into similar-sized wedges.
4. Drizzle with oil and add seasoning.
5. Transfer to the air fryer basket and set the timer for 20 minutes.
6. Check on them at the halfway mark to shake them about.
7. After 20 minutes, they should be crispy on the outside and soft and fluffy on the inside. If they are not, return them to the air fryer and continue cooking, checking on them after 2 minutes.
8. Serve the sweet potato wedges as a side dish or with your favorite dip.

Nutritional Value (Amount per Serving):

Calories: 323
Fat: 3.83 g
Carb: 66.4 g
Protein: 7.89 g

Air Fryer Burger

Preparation Time: 5 Minutes
Cook Time: 8 Minutes

Serves: 2

Ingredients:

- 2 burger patties (fresh or frozen)
- 2 lettuce leaves (optional)
- 2 slices cheese (optional)
- ½ onion, chopped
- 2 burger baps
- 1 tomato, sliced

Directions:

1. Lay the burger patties in the air fryer basket. If you want to cook the onion at the same time you can also add these now.
2. Set the air fryer off at 180°C for 8 minutes.
3. At the 4-minute mark, flip the burger over.
4. At the 8-minute mark check whether the burger is cooked through, the juices should run clear.
5. If you want to turn it into a cheeseburger, lay the slices of cheese over each burger. You can also lightly toast the burger baps at the same time by inserting a trivet and laying them on top of it.
6. Air fry for a further minute, or until the cheese has melted and the baps are lightly toasted.
7. Assemble the burgers in the baps with your choice of salad and sauces.

Nutritional Value (Amount per Serving):

Calories: 1177
Fat: 82.27 g

Carb: 13.89 g
Protein: 90.43 g

Holiday Beef Patties

Preparation Time: 10 Minute
Cook Time: 8 Minutes
Serves: 4

Ingredients:

- 2 tablespoons ham, cut into strips
- 3 tablespoons bread crumbs
- ½ teaspoon nutmeg, ground
- Salt and black pepper to the taste
- 390 g beef, minced
- 1 leek, chopped

Directions:

1. In a bowl, mix beef with leek, salt, pepper, ham, breadcrumbs, and nutmeg.
2. Stir well and shape small patties out of this mix.
3. Place them in your air fryer's basket, and cook at 200°C, for 8 minutes.
4. Arrange them on a platter and serve them as an appetizer.

Nutritional Value (Amount per Serving):

Calories: 260
Fat: 12 g

Carb: 12 g
Protein: 21 g

Air Fryer Halloumi

Preparation Time: 2 Minutes
Cook Time: 8 Minutes
Serves: 8

Ingredients:

- ½ teaspoon dried thyme (optional)
- 1 tablespoons

Directions:

1. Preheat the air fryer to 200°C.
2. Slice halloumi and brush with oil on both sides. Sprinkle with seasoning if using.
3. Transfer halloumi slices to the air fryer basket.
4. Air fry for 8 to 10 minutes, turning over halfway.

5. The halloumi is ready when it has softened and is beginning to turn brown around the edges.

Nutritional Value (Amount per Serving):

Calories: 97　　　　　　　　　　Carb: 2.47 g
Fat: 7.66 g　　　　　　　　　　Protein: 4.62 g

Potato Slices

Preparation Time: 5 Minutes
Cook Time: 18 Minutes
Serves: 4

Ingredients:

- 1 teaspoon dried mixed herbs
- 1 teaspoon garlic granules
- 1 tablespoon olive oil
- 4 large potatoes
- ½ teaspoon salt

Directions:

1. Wash and cut the potatoes into ½ cm slices.
2. Put the sliced potatoes in a pot of water.
3. Drain the water and pat the potatoes dry with kitchen paper or a clean kitchen towel.
4. Add the oil, garlic, herbs, and salt to the dry sliced potatoes, tossing them about until they are all coated.
5. Transfer the sliced potatoes to the air fryer basket and cook at 200°C for 18 minutes, shaking halfway through. The potato slices should be crispy on the outside and soft on the inside. If they are not, return to the air fryer for a further two minutes.
6. Serve as a side dish or as a snack.

Nutritional Value (Amount per Serving):

Calories: 315　　　　　　　　　　Carb: 64.7 g
Fat: 3.71 g　　　　　　　　　　Protein: 7.5 g

Chicken Nuggets

Preparation Time: 10 Minutes
Cook Time: 8 Minutes
Serves: 4

Ingredients:

- 3-4 boneless chicken breasts
- 100 g breadcrumbs
- 2 eggs, beaten

Seasoning of your choice:

- 1 teaspoon smoked paprika
- 1 teaspoon garlic granules
- ½ teaspoon salt
- ½ teaspoon pepper

Directions:

1. Cut chicken breasts up into small chicken nugget-sized chunks.
2. Set up a chicken nugget breading station of three bowls.
3. Add the beaten egg to one bowl, mix the seasoning with the breadcrumbs, add to a different bowl, and put the raw chicken pieces in another bowl.
4. Using kitchen tongs, dip the chicken in the beaten egg, then roll it in the seasoned breadcrumbs. Place in air fryer basket.
5. Repeat with each piece of chicken. Depending on the size of your air fryer, you may need to cook in 2 separate batches.
6. Cook at 200°C for 8 to 10 minutes.
7. Check the chicken nuggets are cooked through before serving.

Nutritional Value (Amount per Serving):

Calories: 767   Protein: 94.01 g
Fat: 40.24 g
Carb: 1.57 g

Carrot Cake

Preparation Time: 10 Minutes
Cook Time: 25 Minutes
Serves: 1

Ingredients:

- 175 g grated carrot (approx 2 medium carrots)
- 1 teaspoon ground cinnamon
- 140 g Soft brown sugar
- 1 orange, zest, and juice
- 200 g self-raising flour
- 2 eggs, beaten
- 140 g butter
- 60 g sultanas

Directions:

1. Preheat the air fryer to 175C.
2. In a bowl, cream together the butter and sugar.
3. Slowly add the beaten eggs.
4. Fold in the flour, a little bit at a time, mixing it as you go.
5. Add the orange juice and zest, grated carrots, and sultanas. Gently mix all the ingredients.
6. Grease the baking tin and pour the mixture in.
7. Place the baking tin in the air fryer basket and cook for 25-30 minutes. Check and see if the cake has cooked - use a cocktail stick or metal skewer to poke in the middle. If it comes out wet then cook it for a little longer.
8. Remove the baking tin from the air fryer basket and allow it to cool for 10 minutes before removing it from the tin.

Nutritional Value (Amount per Serving):

Calories: 2647   Carb: 314.17 g
Fat: 135.17 g   Protein: 41.41 g

rosemary, salt, and pepper, and toss.

2. Introduce in your air fryer and cook at 190°C for 25 minutes.
3. Blend using an immersion blender, divide into bowls, and serve cold.

Nutritional Value (Amount per Serving):

Calories: 182
Fat: 5 g

Carb: 12 g
Protein: 5 g

Shrimp and Calamari Snack

Preparation Time: 20 Minutes
Cook Time: 9 Minutes
Serves: 1

Ingredients:

- 225 g calamari, cut into medium rings
- 200 g shrimp, peeled and deveined
- A splash of Worcestershire sauce
- 2 tablespoons avocado, chopped
- ½ teaspoon turmeric powder
- 1 teaspoon tomato paste
- 1 tablespoon mayonnaise
- 1 teaspoon lemon juice
- 3 tablespoons white flour
- 1 tablespoon olive oil
- 1 egg
- Salt and black pepper to the taste

Directions:

1. In a bowl, whisk the egg with oil, add calamari rings and shrimp, and toss to coat.
2. In another bowl, mix flour with salt, pepper, and turmeric and stir.

3. Dredge calamari and shrimp in this mix, and place them in your air fryer's basket.
4. Cook at 176°C, for 9 minutes, flipping them once.
5. Meanwhile, in a bowl, mix avocado with mayo and tomato paste and mash using a fork.
6. Add Worcestershire sauce, lemon juice, salt, and pepper and stir well.
7. Arrange calamari and shrimp on a platter and serve with the sauce on the side.

Nutritional Value (Amount per Serving):

Calories: 288
Fat: 23 g

Carb: 10 g
Protein: 15 g

Potato and Beans Dip

Preparation Time: 10 Minutes
Cook Time: 10 Minutes
Serves: 10

Ingredients:

- 235 g sweet potatoes, peeled and chopped
- 540 g canned garbanzo beans, drained
- 5 garlic cloves, minced
- ½ teaspoon cumin, ground
- 60 g sesame paste
- 2 tablespoons lemon juice
- 1 tablespoon olive oil
- 2 tablespoons water
- Salt and white pepper to the taste

Directions:

1. Put potatoes in your air fryer's basket.
2. Cook them at 182°C for 10 minutes.

3. Cool them down, peel them, put them in your food processor, and pulse well.
4. Add sesame paste, garlic, beans, lemon juice, cumin, water, oil, salt, and pepper, and pulse again.
5. Divide into bowls, and serve cold.

Nutritional Value (Amount per Serving):

Calories: 170
Fat: 3 g
Carb: 12 g
Protein: 11 g

Chapter 2: Breakfast Recipes

Breakfast Potatoes

Preparation Time: 10 Minutes
Cook Time: 15 Minutes
Serves: 2

Ingredients:

- ½ teaspoon smoked paprika
- 2 x medium/large potatoes
- ½ teaspoon black pepper
- 1 tablespoon olive oil
- ½ teaspoon garlic salt

Directions:

1. Peel and chop potatoes into 1-inch cubes. Use approximately 1 medium to large potato per serving.
2. Preheat the air fryer to 200°C for about 5 minutes
3. Rinse chopped potatoes in water and pat dry with a kitchen towel.
4. Coat potatoes in oil and sprinkle seasoning over them. Stir so that they are all covered.
5. Transfer potatoes to an air fryer basket and cook for 15 minutes. Check on them at the halfway mark and give them a shake.

Tips:

Depending on your air fryer they might take less or more time so keep an eye on them when you first cook them. They are ready when they are golden brown and crispy.

Nutritional Value (Amount per Serving):

Calories: 348
Fat: 7.19 g
Carb: 65.5 g
Protein: 7.66 g

Air Fryer Falafel

Preparation Time: 10 Minutes
Cook Time: 35 Minutes
Serves: 20

Ingredients:

Falafel:

- 2 x 400 g cans chickpeas, rinsed and drained
- ½ medium yellow onion, cut into quarters
- 5 g packed parsley leaves
- 5 g packed coriander leaves
- 1 teaspoon baking powder
- 1 teaspoon dried coriander
- ½ teaspoon chili flakes
- 1 teaspoon salt
- 4 cloves garlic

Tahini Sauce:

- 3 tablespoons water, plus more as needed
- Juice of ½ a lemon
- Pinch of chili flakes
- Pinch of salt
- 80 g tahini

Directions:

1. In a food processor, pulse onion, garlic, parsley, and coriander until roughly chopped, scraping down sides as needed.
2. Add drained chickpeas, salt, baking powder, coriander, cumin, and chili flakes.
3. Pulse again until the chickpeas are mostly broken down with some chunks. You want to stop just before the mixture turns into a paste. Taste and adjust seasonings.
4. Scoop out about 2 tablespoons worth of mixture and gently

form into a ball without squeezing together too much or the falafels will be dense.

5. Working in batches, place falafels in the basket of an air fryer and cook at 190°C for 15 minutes.
6. Meanwhile, make tahini sauce: In a medium bowl, combine tahini and lemon juice.
7. Add water and stir until combined. Add more water 1 tablespoon at a time until desired consistency is reached.
8. Season with a big pinch of salt and chili flakes.
9. Serve falafels as is with sauce, in a salad, or a pitta.

Nutritional Value (Amount per Serving):

Calories: 36
Fat: 2.92 g

Carb: 1.88 g
Protein: 1 g

Two Ingredient Pizza

Preparation Time: 5 Minutes
Cook Time: 10 Minutes
Serves: 2

Ingredients:

- Cheese, grated (enough to sprinkle on 2 small pizzas)
- 240 g natural or Greek yogurt
- 350 g self-raising flour
- Pizza sauce/passata
- Toppings of your choice (pineapple, pepperoni, peppers, chicken, etc.)

Directions:

1. Mix the self-raising flour and yogurt (add more flour if necessary) until a dough consistency has been formed.
2. Split dough in 2.
3. Roll each one out on a floured surface.

4. Place a bit of parchment paper in an air fryer basket and cook at 200°C for 8 to 10 minutes, turning over halfway.
5. Take the pizza out and add pizza sauce, grated cheese, and any other toppings of your choice.
6. Return to the air fryer basket and cook for a further 3 minutes.
7. Repeat with 2nd pizza.

Nutritional Value (Amount per Serving):

Calories: 889
Fat: 8.45 g

Carb: 161.12 g
Protein: 38.49 g

Frozen Sausage Rolls

Preparation Time: 1 Minute
Cook Time: 18 Minutes
Serves: 4

Ingredients:

- 4 large frozen sausage rolls (or 12 mini sausage rolls)
- 1 beaten egg (optional for basting)

Directions:

1. Preheat the air fryer to 180°C.
2. Lay the frozen sausage rolls in the air fryer basket, allowing a bit of space between each one. Optionally baste with some beaten egg or milk. This will help turn the pastry golden.
3. Air fries large sausage rolls for 18 to 20 minutes and mini sausage rolls for 10 to 12 minutes. Check on the sausage rolls at the halfway mark to ensure they are not burning.
4. At the end of the cooking time, the sausage rolls should be golden brown on the outside and piping hot on the inside. If the pastry is still pale, turn the air fryer temperature up to 200°C for 1 to 2 minutes.
5. Leave to rest for a few minutes before eating.

Ingredients:

- 2 portions of roasted tomato pizza sauce
- 60 g grated mozzarella and cheddar mix
- Mixed Italian herbs basil and oregano
- ½ portion of pizza dough

Directions:

1. Roll out the pizza dough as thin as possible.
2. Spread over the tomato pizza sauce.
3. Add the grated cheddar.
4. Sprinkle on ½ of your herbs.
5. Roll up as tightly as possible. I find that using baking paper or cling film works well here.
6. Slice into 2.5cm slices.
7. Pop into the air fryer basket.
8. Bake at 200°C for 6-7 minutes until golden brown.
9. Sprinkle over the remainder of the herbs when serving.

Nutritional Value (Amount per Serving):

Calories: 324
Fat: 11.27 g

Carb: 42.2 g
Protein: 9.79 g

Roast Potatoes

Preparation Time: 5 Minutes
Cook Time: 30 Minutes
Serves: 3

Ingredients:

- 600 g potatoes, peeled, washed and chopped
- ½ tablespoon vegetable oil
- Salt and pepper

Directions:

1. Pre-heat the air fryer to 180°C.
2. Drizzle with the vegetable oil and salt and pepper.
3. Add to the air fryer basket.
4. Cook for 15 minutes at 180°C. Shake well.
5. If you're adding additional herbs, spices, or seasonings now is the time to add these.
6. Cook for another 10 minutes at 180°C. Check. If required cook for a further 5 minutes.

Nutritional Value (Amount per Serving):

Calories: 180
Fat: 2.5 g

Carb: 36.43 g
Protein: 4.26 g

Mashed Potatoes

Preparation Time: 5 Minutes
Cook Time: 25 Minutes
Serves: 3

Ingredients:

- 500 g baby potatoes first early works too
- 15 ml olive oil
- Salt and pepper
- 1 stalk chives
- 20 g butter

Directions:

1. Wash and dry your potatoes.
2. Place the potatoes on a piece of tin foil
3. Cover with 15 ml of olive oil, and sprinkle generously with salt and pepper. Wrap up the foil over the potatoes.
4. Air fryer at 200°C for 20 minutes.
5. Once the time is up ensure that the potatoes are fork-tender. If not then you'll want to cook for 3-5 minutes more.

6. Once your potatoes are cooked through remove them and place them in a bowl.
7. Add 20 g of butter and mash until smooth.
8. Season with salt and pepper. Chop a stalk of chives and scatter on the top.
9. If you're serving family style then smooth the top and dab 10 g of butter on to give it a nice presentation.

Nutritional Value (Amount per Serving):

Calories: 427

Carb: 37.18 g

Fat: 29.21 g

Protein: 8.59 g

Potato Wedges

Preparation Time: 5 Minutes
Cook Time: 20 Minutes
Serves: 2

Ingredients:

- 400 g Potatoes, washed, peeled if desired
- Spray oil

Optional dressings:

- Garlic and parsley – mince together 2 garlic cloves 15 g butter (melted) and 1 teaspoon chopped parsley
- Cajun seasoning

Directions:

1. Preheat your air fryer to 160°C.
2. Cut potatoes in half. Then cut into quarters.
3. Slice diagonally to make 3-4 wedges from each quarter.
4. Rinse in cold water.
5. Pat them dry on a clean towel or using a kitchen towel.
6. Spray with oil and add your optional dressing, if required.

7. Alternatively you can use 1 teaspoon of salt and pepper and lightly coat with spray oil.
8. Cook for 12 minutes at 160°C in your air fryer.
9. Turn up to 200°C for around 6-8 minutes. Check after 5 minutes as depending on size they can cook quickly.

Nutritional Value (Amount per Serving):

Calories: 389
Fat: 5.01 g
Carb: 81.9 g
Protein: 5.7 g

drumettes from the wingettes.

2. If you're keeping things simple and just using the hot sauce, you can skip this step. Mix up your sauce by combining the hot sauce, melted butter, brown sugar, and Worcestershire sauce. The butter will make the wings nice and decadent while the brown sugar and Worcestershire sauce will add some depth to the flavor.

3. You can play around with how much of these extra ingredients you add to the hot sauce. Taste test until you get the right flavor. You can also try adding some spices like cayenne pepper and garlic powder for that extra kick.

4. Pour half of the sauce over the wings and stir to make sure the wings are well-covered. For especially flavorful and tender wings, let this marinate in the refrigerator for at least a few hours or even overnight – this will allow more of the sauce to be absorbed.

5. Put the wings into the air fryer basket, set the temperature to 380 degrees, and cook the wings for 20 minutes.

6. After 20 minutes, remove the fry basket and give it a good shake to ensure even cooking, you can also use tongs to turn the wings instead of shaking.

7. Turn the temperature up to 400 degrees and cook the wings for another 5 minutes.

8. Remove the wings and coat with the remaining hot sauce then serve.

Nutritional Value (Amount per Serving):

Calories: 1603
Fat: 32.76 g
Carb: 263.29 g
Protein: 115.17 g

Cajun Chicken

Preparation Time: 5 Minutes
Cook Time: 20 Minutes
Serves: 4

Ingredients:

- Cajun seasoning see my recipe
- 640 g chicken mini fillets

Directions:

1. Add your chicken to a bowl.
2. Add your cajun seasoning and rub it all over the chicken fillets.
3. Lightly oil the air fryer basket (if desired – I use spray rapeseed oil)
4. Add your chicken mini fillets to the air fryer.
5. Cook at 200°C for 20 minutes, turning 10 minutes in.
6. If you overload the air fryer basket a little, like me, then you'll want to give these a shake a couple of times during the 20 minutes.
7. Check the temperature before serving. Chicken should be at least 74°C internally before serving.

Nutritional Value (Amount per Serving):

Calories: 462
Fat: 18.08 g

Carb: 51.76 g
Protein: 22.3 g

Chicken Tenders

Preparation Time: 15 Minutes
Cook Time: 45 Minutes
Serves: 4

Ingredients:

The Chicken Tenders:

- Freshly ground black pepper
- 250 g panko bread crumbs
- 675 g chicken tenders
- 195 g plain flour
- 60 ml buttermilk
- Cooking spray
- 2 large eggs
- Salt

The Honey Mustard:

- ¼ teaspoon hot sauce (optional)
- 2 tablespoon Dijon mustard
- Freshly ground black pepper
- 3 tablespoons honey
- 80 g mayonnaise
- Pinch of salt

Directions:

1. Season chicken tenders on both sides with salt and pepper.
2. Place flour and bread crumbs in two separate shallow bowls.
3. In a third bowl, whisk together eggs and buttermilk.
4. Working one at a time, dip chicken in flour, then egg mixture, and finally in bread crumbs, pressing to coat.
5. Working in batches, place chicken tenders in the basket of the air fryer, being sure to not overcrowd it.
6. Spray the tops of the chicken with cooking spray and cook at 200°C for 5 minutes.
7. Flip the chicken over, spray the tops with more cooking spray, and cook for 5 minutes more. Repeat with remaining chicken tenders.
8. Make the sauce: In a small bowl, whisk together mayonnaise, honey, dijon, and hot sauce, if using. Season with a pinch of salt and a few cracks of black pepper.
9. Serve chicken tenders with honey mustard.

Nutritional Value (Amount per Serving):

Calories: 962
Fat: 29.37 g

Carb: 89.03 g
Protein: 80.45 g

Rotisserie Chicken

Preparation Time: 20 Minutes
Cook Time: 50 Minutes
Serves: 6

Ingredients:

- 1 (1.3kg.) chicken, cut into 8 pieces
- Freshly ground black pepper
- 1 tablespoon dried thyme
- 2 teaspoons dried oregano
- 2 teaspoons garlic powder
- 2 teaspoon onion powder
- 1 teaspoon smoked paprika
- ¼ teaspoon cayenne
- Salt

Directions:

1. Season chicken pieces all over with salt and pepper.
2. In a medium bowl, whisk to combine herbs and spices, then rub the spice mix all over the chicken pieces.
3. Add dark meat pieces to the air fryer basket and cook at 180°C for 10 minutes, then flip and cook 10 minutes more.
4. Repeat with chicken breasts, but reduce time to 8 minutes per side. Use a meat thermometer to ensure that chicken is cooked through, each piece should register 73°C.

Nutritional Value (Amount per Serving):

Calories: 340
Fat: 15.23 g
Carb: 1.97 g
Protein: 46.1 g

Nutritional Value (Amount per Serving):

Calories: 1803
Fat: 118.5 g

Carb: 3.96 g
Protein: 169.98 g

Chicken Parmesan

Preparation Time: 10 Minutes
Cook Time: 40 Minutes
Serves: 4

Ingredients:

- Freshly chopped parsley, for garnish
- 2 large boneless chicken breasts
- 240 g marinara/tomato sauce
- Freshly ground black pepper
- 25 g freshly grated Parmesan
- 100 g panko bread crumbs
- 1 teaspoon dried oregano
- ½ teaspoon garlic powder
- ½ teaspoon chili flakes
- 100 g grated mozzarella
- 40 g plain flour
- 2 large eggs
- Salt

Directions:

1. Carefully butterfly chicken by cutting it in half widthwise to create 4 thin pieces of chicken.
2. Season on both sides with salt and pepper.
3. Prepare dredging station: Place flour in a shallow bowl and season with a large pinch of salt and pepper. Place eggs in a second bowl and beat. In a third bowl, combine bread crumbs, Parmesan, oregano, garlic powder, and chili flakes.

4. Working with one piece of chicken at a time, coat in flour, then dip in eggs, and finally press into panko mixture making sure both sides are coated well.
5. Working in batches as necessary, place chicken in the basket of an air fryer and cook at 200°C for 5 minutes on each side.
6. Top chicken with sauce and mozzarella and cook at 200°C for 3 minutes more or until cheese is melty and golden.
7. Garnish with parsley to serve.

Nutritional Value (Amount per Serving):

Calories: 633
Fat: 23.16 g

Carb: 37.03 g
Protein: 63.72 g

BBQ Chicken Breast

Preparation Time: 3 Minutes
Cook Time: 20 Minutes
Serves: 2

Ingredients:

- 2 chicken breasts 1 per person
- Garlic salt or garlic powder
- Salt and pepper
- Smoked paprika
- 80 ml BBQ sauce
- Spray oil

Directions:

1. Spray your chicken breasts with spray oil.
2. Sprinkle over smoked paprika, and garlic salt and season well with salt and pepper too. Alternatively, you can mix it all together beforehand and sprinkle it on.
3. Turn over and repeat this step.
4. Lay the chicken in the air fryer basket.

5. Cook at 180°C for 10 minutes. Turn over the chicken breast. Cook at 180°C for another 8 minutes.
6. Pour over the barbecue sauce, I like to use a silicone pastry brush to ensure even coverage, but you can just use a spoon or whatever you have to hand.
7. Cook at 180°C for another 2 minutes.
8. Check the internal temperature of the chicken breast (in the thickest part) is a minimum of 74C and then remove it.
9. You can rest for 5 minutes before you slice and serve. Or just serve up as a whole chicken breast alongside the rest of your dinner.

Nutritional Value (Amount per Serving):

Calories: 477
Fat: 15.95 g

Carb: 80.18 g
Protein: 20.21 g

Spicy Chicken Thighs

Preparation Time: 10 Minutes
Cook Time: 1 Hour 10 Minutes
Serves: 4

Ingredients:

- Thinly sliced spring onions, for garnish
- Toasted sesame seeds, for garnish
- 2 teaspoons freshly grated ginger
- 4 bone-in, skin-on chicken thighs
- 2 tablespoons chili garlic sauce
- 80 ml low-sodium soy sauce
- 60 ml extra-virgin olive oil
- 2 cloves garlic, crushed
- 2 tablespoons honey
- Juice of 1 lime

Directions:

1. In a large bowl, combine soy sauce, oil, honey, chili garlic sauce, lime juice, garlic, and ginger. Reserve 120 ml cup of marinade.
2. Add chicken thighs to the bowl and toss to coat. Cover and refrigerate for at least 30 minutes.
3. Remove 2 thighs from the marinade and place them in the basket of the air fryer.
4. Cook at 200°C until thighs are cooked through to an internal temperature of 73°C, 15 to 20 minutes.
5. Transfer thighs to a plate and tent with foil. Repeat with remaining thighs.
6. Meanwhile, in a small saucepan over medium heat, bring the reserved marinade to a boil.
7. Reduce heat and simmer until sauce thickens slightly 4 to 5 minutes.
8. Brush sauce over thighs and garnish with spring onions and sesame seeds before serving.

Nutritional Value (Amount per Serving):

Calories: 3902
Fat: 373.13 g
Carb: 46.35 g
Protein: 96.87 g

Calories: 491   Carb: 1 g
Fat: 34 g   Protein: 46 g

Crispy Air Fryer Bacon

Preparation Time: 5 Minutes
Cook Time: 10 Minutes
Serves: 8

Ingredients:

- 340 g thick-cut bacon

Directions:

1. Lay bacon inside the air fryer basket in a single layer.
2. Set the air fryer to 200°C and cook until crispy, about 10 minutes. (You can check halfway through and rearrange slices with tongs.)

Nutritional Value (Amount per Serving):

Calories: 132   Carb: 2.69 g
Fat: 12.55 g   Protein: 4.54 g

Air Fryer Steak

Preparation Time: 5 Minutes
Cook Time: 8 Minutes
Serves: 1

Ingredients:

- Sirloin steak (or your favorite cut of steak)
- Oil (optional)

- Seasoning

1. Take the steak out of the fridge and leave it out for at least 30 minutes so that it can get to room temperature.
2. Preheat the air fryer to 200°C.
3. Optionally rub some oil on both sides of the steak and season according to taste.
4. Place in the air fryer - either on a trivet or directly on the base of the air fryer basket.
5. Set the air fryer timer to your desired time, depending on how well you want it cooked.
6. Turn the steak over halfway through.
7. At the end of the cooking time check the steak is cooked to your liking remove it from the air fryer and leave it to rest for at least 5 minutes.

Nutritional Value (Amount per Serving):

Calories: 795

Carb: 1.68 g

Fat: 40.15 g

Protein: 91.76 g

Lamb Chops

Preparation Time: 5 Minutes
Cook Time: 10 Minutes
Serves: 6

Ingredients:

- 3 tablespoons fresh Parsley minced or ½ tablespoon dried
- 2 tablespoons Lemon juice or cider vinegar
- ½ teaspoon Black pepper
- 3 cloves Garlic minced
- 2 tablespoons Olive oil
- ½ teaspoon Oregano

- 700 g Lamb chops
- Salt to taste

Directions:

1. Pat dry the chops with a paper towel and add to a bowl. cut lamb in a bowl.
2. Add parsley, oregano, black pepper, garlic, lemon juice, olive oil, and salt. Mix till well combined.
3. You can put it in the fridge to marinate for 30-60 minutes but if you don't have time for that, move to the next step.
4. Other ingredients are added to the bowl.
5. Preheat the Air fryer to a temperature of 200°C for 5 minutes.
6. Seasoned lamb arranged in an air fryer basket.
7. Insert the basket in the air fryer and air fry lamb chops for 5 minutes.
8. After 5 minutes flip the chops to the other side and cook for another 5 minutes (This time is for well-done lamb as I like it.
9. Bring out the cooked lamb and serve.

Nutritional Value (Amount per Serving):

Calories: 240
Fat: 13 g

Carb: 1 g
Protein: 29 g

Pork Chops

Preparation Time: 5 Minutes
Cook Time: 12 Minutes
Serves: 1

Ingredients:

- ½ tablespoon seasoning (see notes)
- ½ tablespoon olive oil
- 1 pork chop

Directions:

1. Preheat the air fryer to 200°C.
2. Brush oil on each side of the pork chop.
3. Add seasoning and rub it in evenly all over.
4. Place pork chop in the preheated air fryer and set the timer for 12 minutes.
5. Turn the pork chop over at around the 6-minute mark.
6. Check the pork chop is cooked all the way through - it should be golden brown on the outside and juices should run clear.

Nutritional Value (Amount per Serving):

Calories: 402
Fat: 24.16 g
Carb: 2.49 g
Protein: 40.4 g

Chapter 5: Vegetable Recipes

Air Fryer Parsnips

Preparation Time: 5 Minutes
Cook Time: 15 Minutes
Serves: 4

Ingredients:

- Salt and pepper to taste
- 4 medium parsnips
- 1 tablespoon oil

Directions:

1. Top and tail the parsnips. Optionally peel the parsnips.
2. Drizzle oil over the parsnips and toss until they are covered.
3. Season with salt and pepper according to taste.
4. Transfer the parsnips to the air fryer basket.
5. Set the temperature to 200°C and air fry for 15 minutes.
6. Shake the air fryer basket at the halfway mark.
7. The parsnips will be soft in the middle and golden brown on the outside when they are ready, if necessary, air fry for longer.

Nutritional Value (Amount per Serving):

Calories: 107
Fat: 3.88 g

Carb: 16.49 g
Protein: 3.31 g

Brussel Sprouts

Preparation Time: 10 Minutes
Cook Time: 15 Minutes
Serves: 4

Ingredients:

- 2 tablespoons parmesan cheese (optional)

- 400 g Brussels sprouts, halved
- ½ teaspoon garlic granules
- Salt and pepper to season
- 200 g bacon lardons

Directions:

1. Slice the Brussels sprouts in half and place them in a bowl.
2. Sprinkle the garlic granules over them and optionally salt and pepper.
3. Toss the sprouts about so that they all get covered.
4. Add the bacon lardons and mix in.
5. Transfer to the air fryer basket and cook at 180°C for 15 to 20 minutes.
6. Check on them halfway through and give them a shake. They are ready when they are soft on the inside and browned on the outside.
7. Optionally sprinkle with cheese, either 1 minute before the end of the cooking time or while they are still hot so that the cheese can melt a little bit.

Nutritional Value (Amount per Serving):

Calories: 214
Fat: 15.78 g

Carb: 13.64 g
Protein: 9.68 g

Carrot Fries

Preparation Time: 5 Minutes
Cook Time: 15 Minutes
Serves: 2

Ingredients:

- 1 tablespoon of cornflour
- ½ tablespoon of olive oil
- Salt and pepper

- 1 garlic clove
- 3 carrots

Directions:

1. Top and tail your carrots, then peel them if desired.
2. Slice lengthways and then slice lengthways again. (Alternatively, use a potato chipper. These are designed for root vegetables, although I do find carrots very hard so sometimes they get stuck!)
3. Roll the carrot fries in the cornflour and season with salt and pepper.
4. Place in the air fryer basket. Try to avoid overlapping as you want to leave lots of room for air distribution for even cooking to occur.
5. Cook at 200°C for 12 minutes initially. Halfway through pour the oil onto the fries and shake well then continue cooking.
7. If required you can cook for an additional 3-4 minutes.
8. 15-16 minutes is usually sufficient time to cook well, but this WILL depend on the size of the fries that you have cut. Try to aim for even cutting, to ensure cooking.
9. Once cooked I love to serve it alongside a tasty sriracha mayo.

Nutritional Value (Amount per Serving):

Calories: 98　　　　　　　　　Carb: 15.35 g
Fat: 3.95 g　　　　　　　　　　Protein: 1.77 g

Garlic and Herb Potatoes

Preparation Time: 5 Minutes
Cook Time: 20 Minutes

Ingredients:

- 2 tablespoons garlic granules/powder
- 2 tablespoons of olive oil

- Handful of fresh parsley
- 2-3 sprigs rosemary
- 1kg new potatoes
- 2 teaspoon salt

Directions:

1. Chop the potatoes into even-sized chunks, halving the medium ones and quartering the large ones.
2. Finely chop the parsley and the rosemary (leaves only).
3. Place the potatoes in a large bowl, and sprinkle over the chopped herbs, garlic granules, and salt.
4. Drizzle over with olive oil and mix until all potatoes are well-coated.
5. Cook in an air fryer at 200°C for 20 minutes, shaking after 10 minutes.

Tips:

If you have a smaller air fryer, you may have to cook for longer or in 2 small batches.

Nutritional Value (Amount per Serving):

Calories: 1077
Fat: 28.2 g

Carb: 189.39 g
Protein: 23.52 g

Artichokes and Mayonnaise

Preparation Time: 5 Minute
Cook Time: 15 Minutes
Serves: 6

Ingredients:

- 450 g parmesan cheese, grated
- 395 g canned artichoke hearts
- A drizzle of olive oil

- 3 garlic cloves, minced
- 120 g mayonnaise
- 1 teaspoon garlic powder

Directions:

1. In a pan that fits your air fryer, mix the artichokes with the oil, garlic, and garlic powder, and then toss well.
2. Place the pan in the fryer and cook at 176°C for 15 minutes.
3. Cool the mix down, add the mayo, and toss.
4. Divide between plates, sprinkle the parmesan on top, and serve.

Nutritional Value (Amount per Serving):

Calories: 200   Carb: 9 g
Fat: 11 g   Protein: 4 g

Hasselback Potatoes

Preparation Time: 5 Minutes
Cook Time: 30 Minutes
Serves: 4

Ingredients:

- Garlic butter – to make this you'll need butter
- 4 medium potatoes
- Salt and pepper
- Spray oil

Directions:

1. Slice your potatoes ¾ of the way through. Be sure to use a sharp knife and do not slice through the potato.
2. Use spray oil on the potatoes. Season with salt and pepper.
3. Brush each of the slices on both sides using melted garlic butter.

4. Cook at 180°C for 15 minutes.
5. Remove using tongs. Place on a chopping board.
6. Completely baste/brush all of the slices again.
7. Cook at 180°C for another 10 minutes.
8. Brush/baste the potatoes again.
9. Cook at 180°C for another 5-10 minutes, depending on the size.

Nutritional Value (Amount per Serving):

Calories: 301
Fat: 1.7 g

Carb: 65.58 g
Protein: 7.62 g

Zucchini with Mozzarella

Preparation Time: 10 Minute
Cook Time: 15 Minutes
Serves: 6

Ingredients:

- 510 g mozzarella ball, pulled into large pieces
- 3 medium zucchinis, sliced lengthwise
- 3 tablespoons extra virgin olive oil
- Salt and ground black pepper
- ¼ crushed red pepper
- 1 tablespoon lemon juice
- 2 tablespoons fresh dill

Directions:

1. Preheat the air fryer to 176°C
2. Place the grill pan accessory in the air fryer.
3. Drizzle the zucchini with olive oil and season with salt and pepper to taste.
4. Place on the grill pan and cook for 15 to 20 minutes.
5. Serve the zucchini with mozzarella, dill, red pepper, and lemon

juice.

Nutritional Value (Amount per Serving):

Calories: 182 Protein: 11.4 g
Carb: 18.3 g Fat: 7.1 g

Grilled Asparagus with Sauce

Preparation Time: 10 Minute
Cook Time: 15 Minutes
Serves: 6

Ingredients:

- 1360 g asparagus spears, trimmed
- A punch of ground white pepper
- A pinch of mustard powder
- 1 teaspoon chopped tarragon leaves
- 110 g butter, melted
- 2 tablespoons olive oil
- ½ teaspoon salt
- ¼ teaspoon black pepper
- 3 egg yolks
- ½ lemon juice
- ½ teaspoon salt

Directions:

1. Preheat the air fryer to 176°C
2. Place the grill pan accessory in the air fryer.
3. In a Ziploc bag, combine the asparagus, olive oil, salt, and pepper. Give a good shake to combine everything.
4. Dump onto the grill pan and cook for 15 minutes.
5. Meanwhile, on a double boiler over medium flame, whisk the egg yolks, lemon juice, and salt until silky.

- ⅛ teaspoon of white sugar
- 1 white onion

Directions:

1. Chop off both ends of your onion and peel away the skin.
2. Cut the onion in half.
3. Slice each half into semi-circle shapes, around ½ cm thick.
4. Lightly dress the onions with your oil. Don't add the sugar yet.
5. Lay the onions in the air fryer basket, or underneath if you're cooking other items at the same time.
6. Cook at 150°C for 6 minutes, stirring halfway through.
7. Add the sugar and mix well to ensure all the onions have a little coating.
8. Cook at 150°C for another 8 minutes, stirring halfway through.

Tips:

If you want grilled caramelized-style onions then you can remove them now.

If you want very crispy onions then you can continue cooking for another 4-5 minutes, at 150°C, until they are super crispy.

Nutritional Value (Amount per Serving):

Calories: 55
Fat: 4.57 g

Carb: 3.52 g
Protein: 0.4 g

Simple Green Beans

Preparation Time: 2 Minutes
Cook Time: 6 Minutes
Serves: 1

Ingredients:

- 80 g green beans per person
- Salt and pepper

- Spray oil

1. Wash your green beans thoroughly.
2. Top and tail your green beans.
3. Dry completely. (I like to use a clean tea towel for this)
4. Add to a bowl. Use a few sprays of spray oil.
5. Add salt and pepper. Toss gently to ensure even coverage.
6. Pre-heat your air fryer to 200°C.
7. Add the green beans to the air fryer basket.
8. Cook for 6 minutes. Stirring at least once during cooking.
9. If you want extra crispy green beans then you can increase the cooking time to 8 minutes, but do check back at 7 minutes to ensure the beans aren't overcooking.

Nutritional Value (Amount per Serving):

Calories: 392
Fat: 39.12 g

Carb: 10.32 g
Protein: 1.91 g

Grille Tomatoes with Herb Salad

Preparation Time: 10 Minute
Cook Time: 20 Minutes
Serves: 4

Ingredients:

- 60 g hazelnuts, toasted and chopped
- 60 g pistachios, toasted and chopped
- 2 tablespoons white balsamic vinegar
- 175 g cilantro leaves, chopped
- 175 g fresh parsley, chopped
- 120 g chopped chives
- 60 g golden raisins
- 3 large green tomatoes

Air Fryer Cookies

Preparation Time: 10 Minutes
Cook Time: 5 Minutes
Serves: 24

Ingredients:

- ½ teaspoon bicarbonate of soda
- 175 g chocolate chunks or chips
- 70 g light brown sugar
- 10 ml vanilla extract
- 135 g salted butter
- 1 medium egg
- 225 g plain flour
- A pinch of salt
- 70 g sugar

Directions:

1. Beat the butter and both sugars together in a bowl. Once mixed add the egg and vanilla extract.
2. In a separate bowl combine the flour, bicarbonate of soda, salt, and chocolate chunks (or chips!).
3. Add the dry ingredients to the wet ingredients and mix until combined well.
4. Roll the dough into a long sausage shape and chill for a minimum of 1 hour ideally. This will help to make for a more delicious chewy cookie. On occasion, I've left the dough overnight and the cookies are even better!
5. Roll out your cookie dough. I've experimented with balls, lightly pressing down with a fork, molding cookie shapes and just cutting off a little slab from the chilled dough and they all take a very similar time to cook, with similar results, so just be lazy and cut a slab off if you fancy!
6. Pre-heat your air fryer to 180°C for 1-2 minutes if required.

7. Cut a piece of parchment paper to fit the bottom of your air fryer. Without this, the cookie dough may mold to the shape of the bottom of your basket and it will be a nightmare to get it out without it breaking up!
8. I lightly sprayed the parchment paper with 1 calorie spray oil but I think you could get away with skipping this step if you don't have any in.
9. Cook for 5 minutes. Transfer to a wire cooling rack. Gently peel back the parchment paper and you can enjoy your cookies while they are still warm, or they'll keep for 2-3 days in an airtight container.

Tips:

If you're in a hurry you could skip the chilling, but I really feel it adds to the overall texture of the cookies so try to make time!

Nutritional Value (Amount per Serving):

Calories: 174

Fat: 6.98 g

Carb: 19.54 g

Protein: 1.6 g

Dessert Pizza

Preparation Time: 5 Minutes
Cook Time: 5 Minutes
Serves: 8

Ingredients:

- 150 ml chocolate spread
- 150 g strawberries
- Mint to garnish
- 1 pizza base

Directions:

1. Oil the air fryer basket lightly.

Air Fryer Pizookie

Preparation Time: 5 Minutes
Cook Time: 5 Minutes
Serves: 8

Ingredients:

- 175 g chocolate chunks or chocolate chips
- 135 g salted room-temperature butter
- ½ teaspoon bicarbonate of soda
- 70 g light brown sugar
- 10 ml vanilla extract
- 225 g of plain flour
- 70 g sugar
- 1 egg

Directions:

1. Combine the butter and both sugars in a bowl. Add the egg and vanilla extract once combined.
2. In a separate bowl mix together the flour, bicarbonate of soda, and chocolate chunks/chocolate chips.
3. Combine the wet and dry ingredients in a bowl and mix until just combined.
4. Once the dough is mixed roll it out into a circular shape, wrap it in clingfilm, and then chill for a minimum of 1 hour. You can leave it overnight if you'd prefer. Chilling like this helps for a chewier more delicious cookie. (If you're in a hurry you could skip the chilling.)
5. Add the dry ingredients to the wet ingredients and mix until combined well. I like to make either 4 mini cookies with this dough OR one large one, that will serve 8 people comfortably.
6. Take your chilled cookie dough, roll it out, and then shape it to fit either a cake pan or a cast iron skillet. I love to use a well-seasoned cast iron skillet, as I feel this gives a great result with

a chewy cookie with a well-cooked bottom.

7. Pre-heat your air fryer to 180°C for 1-2 minutes if you'd like. I like to do this so the air fryer is ready to go right away.

8. Add your skillet, cake pan, or even just the dough to a baking paper-lined air fryer basket, and then cook for 5 minutes at 180°C.

9. Remove from the air fryer and then transfer to a wire cooling rack to cool down.

Tips:

If you used parchment paper then gently peel this back once it's cooled lightly and it'll keep for 2-3 days.

Nutritional Value (Amount per Serving):

Calories: 531
Fat: 21.62 g
Carb: 58.7 g
Protein: 5.23 g

Chapter 7: Wraps and Sandwiches Recipes

Ham Hock Calzone Pizza

Preparation Time: 10 Minutes
Cook Time: 30 Minutes
Serves: 4

Ingredients:

- 1 medium onion, halved and sliced
- ½ teaspoon dried Italian herbs
- 2 x 220 g frozen ready-made
- 180 g shredded ham hock
- Pizza dough, defrosted
- 1 tablespoon olive oil
- Salt and black pepper
- ¼ teaspoon sugar
- Flour for rolling
- 150 g mozzarella
- 1 clove garlic
- 300 ml passata
- Olive oil spray

Directions:

1. For the filling, heat the oil in a small saucepan, add the garlic and onion, and fry for 5 minutes until the onion has softened, then add the passata, sugar, and dried herbs.
2. Bring to a boil and cook for about 3 minutes, until the sauce has reduced and thickened. Stir in the ham, season, then set aside to cool a little.
3. Divide the pizza dough into 4 equal-sized pieces, then roll each piece into an 18cm circle on a lightly floured surface.
4. Divide the filling mixture between the circles, keeping the filling on one side of the circle.
5. Top with the mozzarella, then wet the edges of the dough with a little water. Fold the calzone, pulling the side without the

Printed in Great Britain
by Amazon